Ss

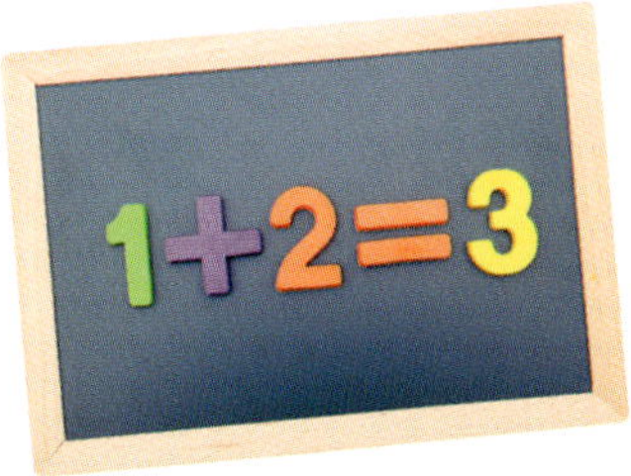

Ransom

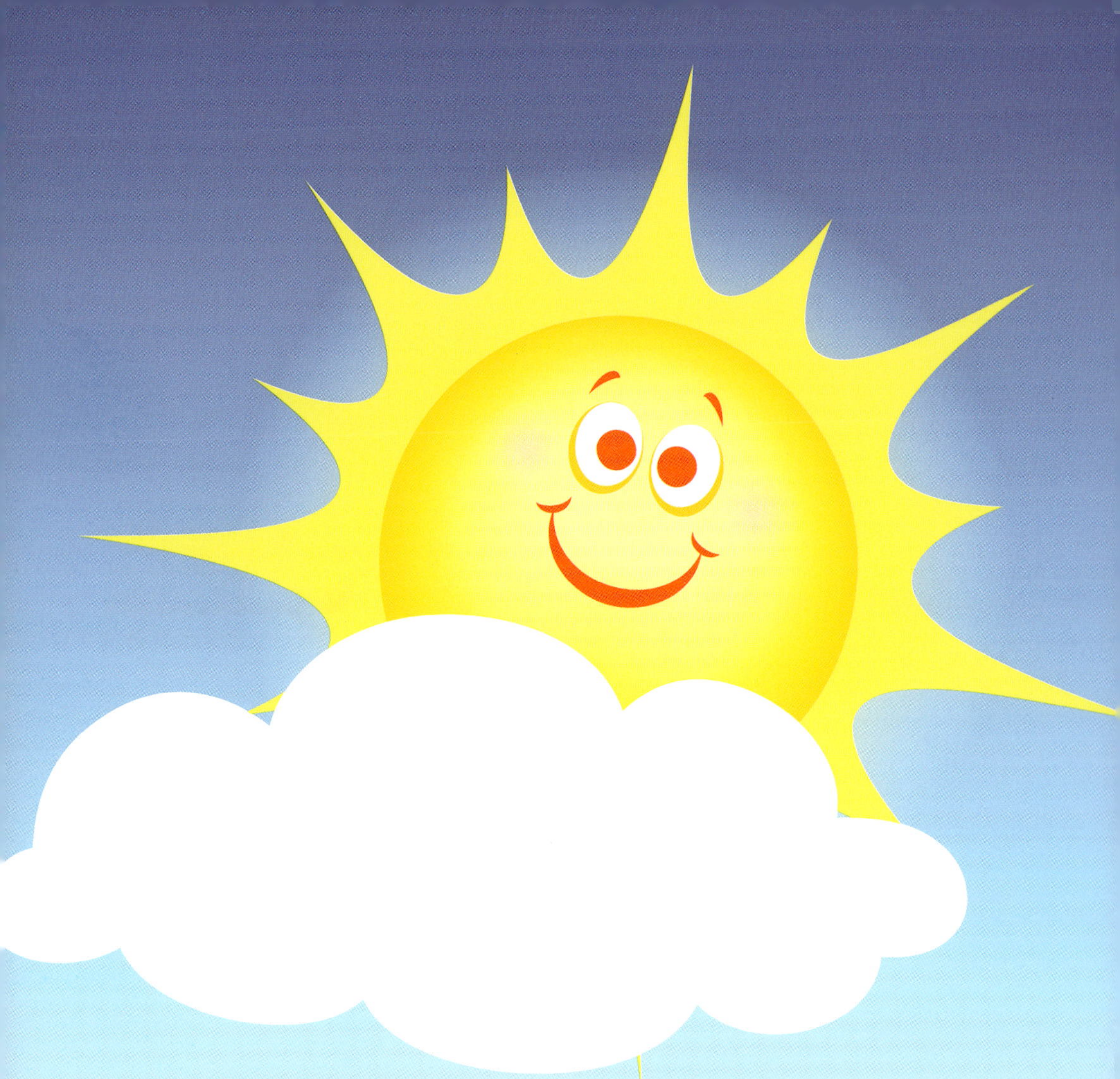

sun

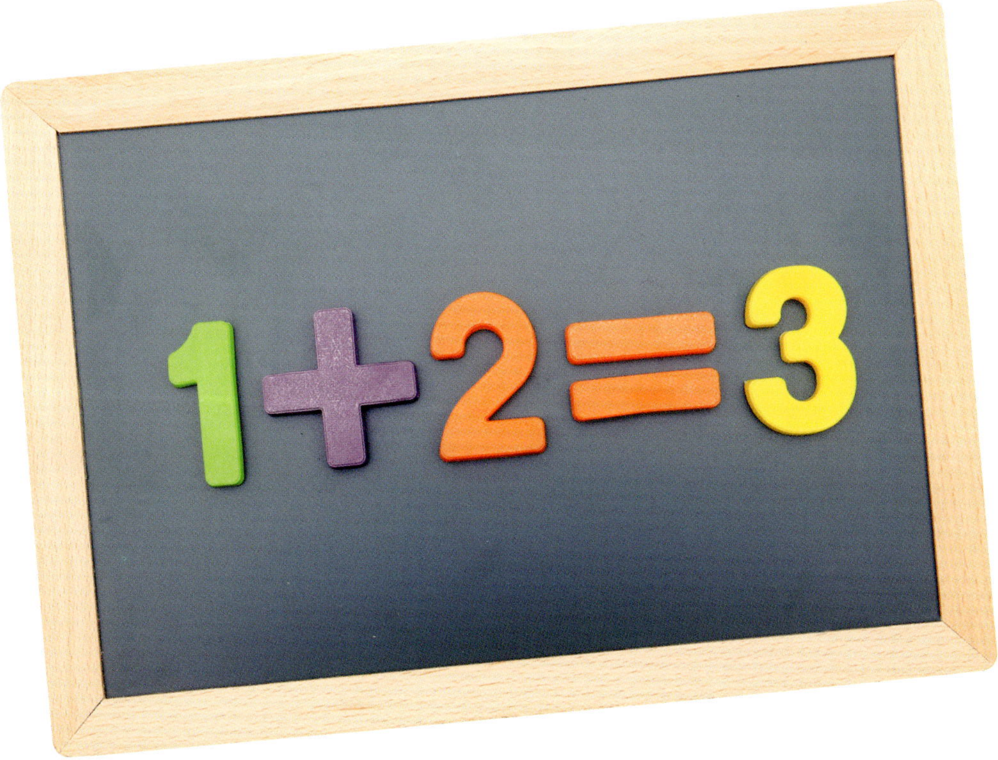

sum

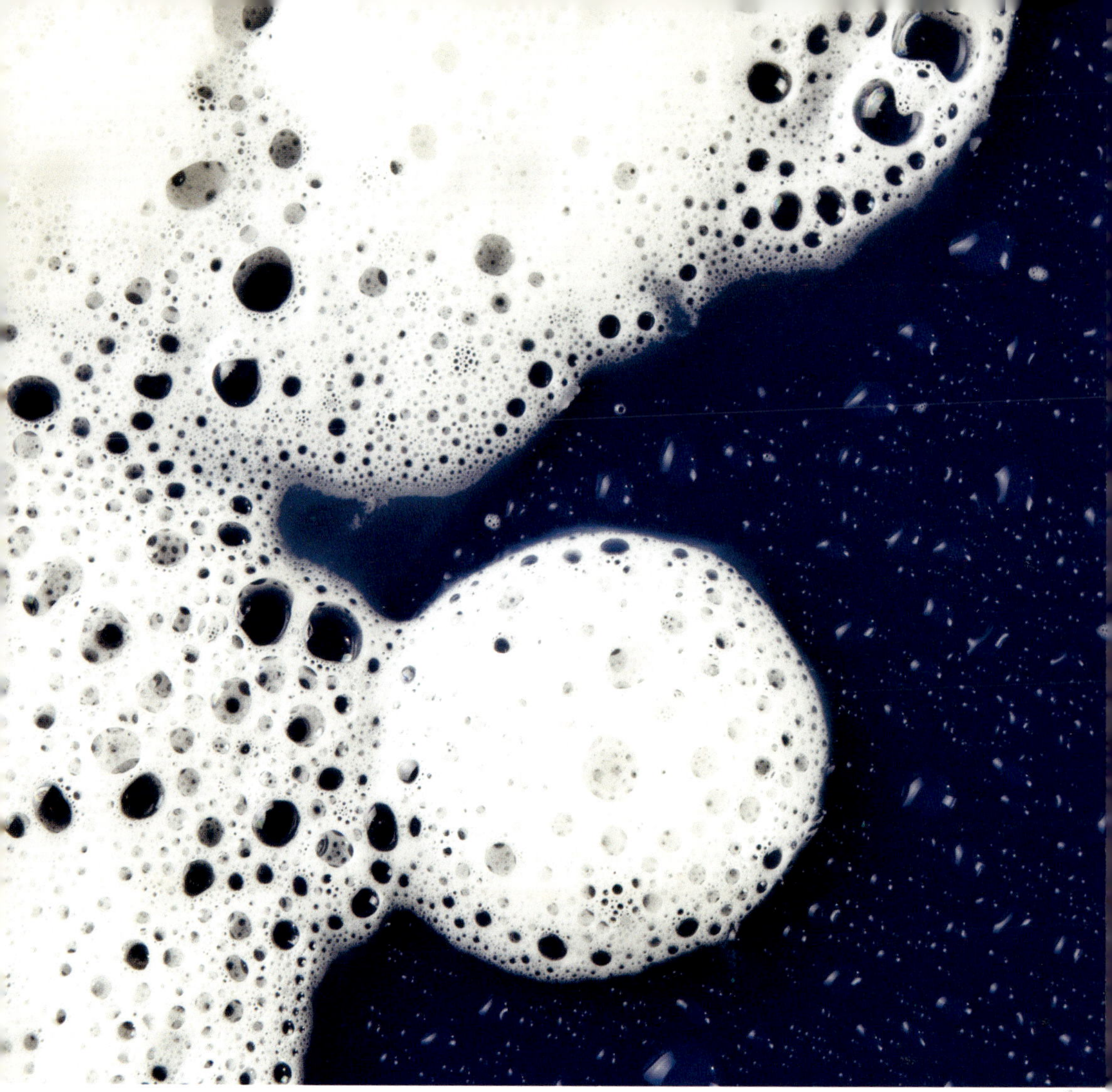

suds

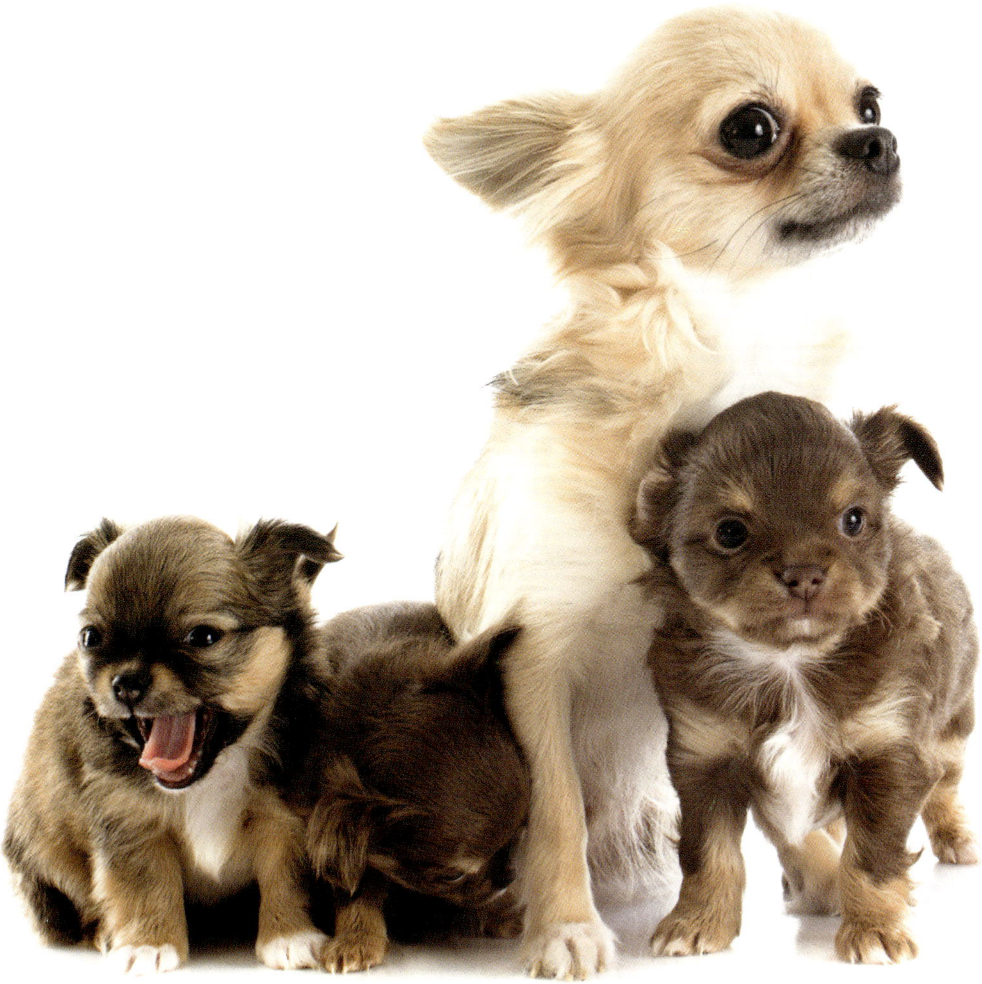

dogs

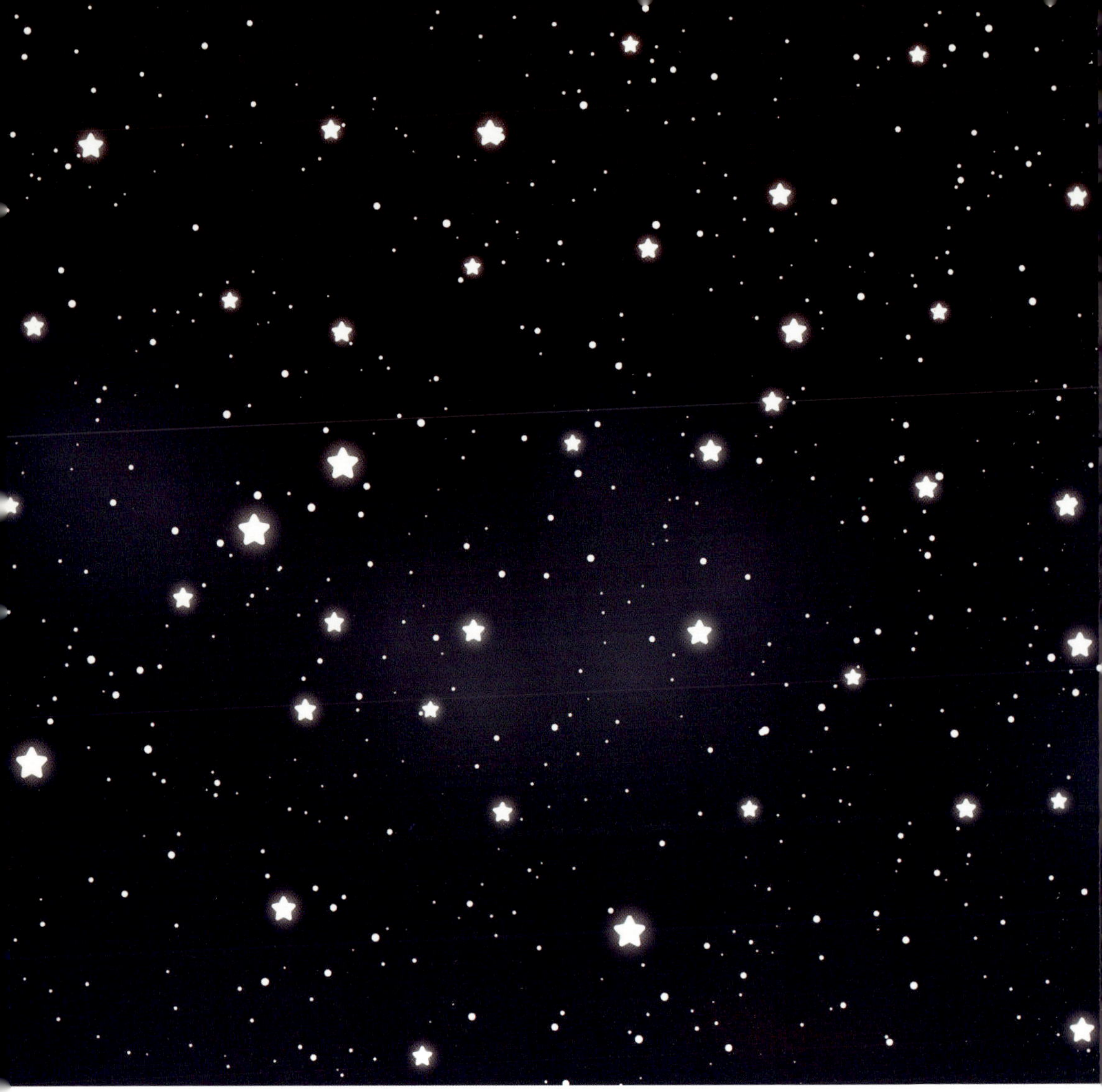

stars

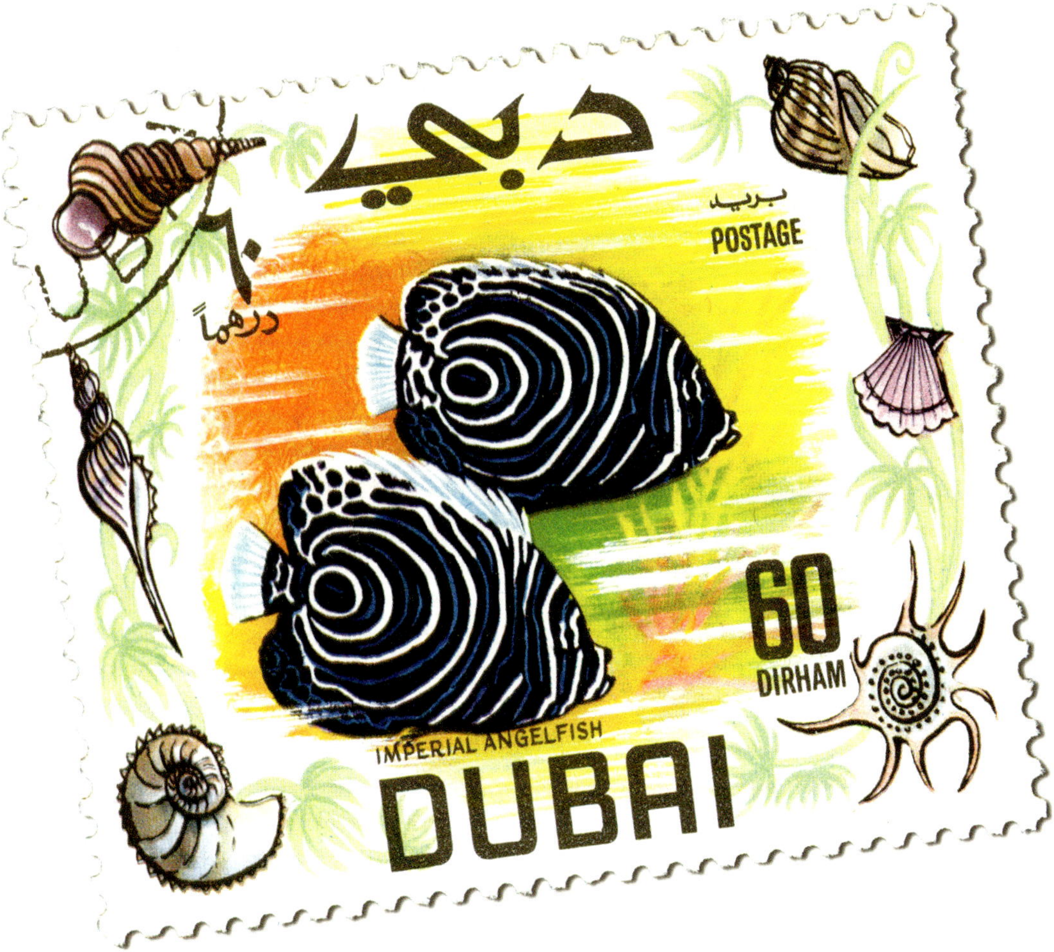
دبي
بريد
POSTAGE
٦٠
درهماً
60
DIRHAM
IMPERIAL ANGELFISH
DUBAI

stamp

sky

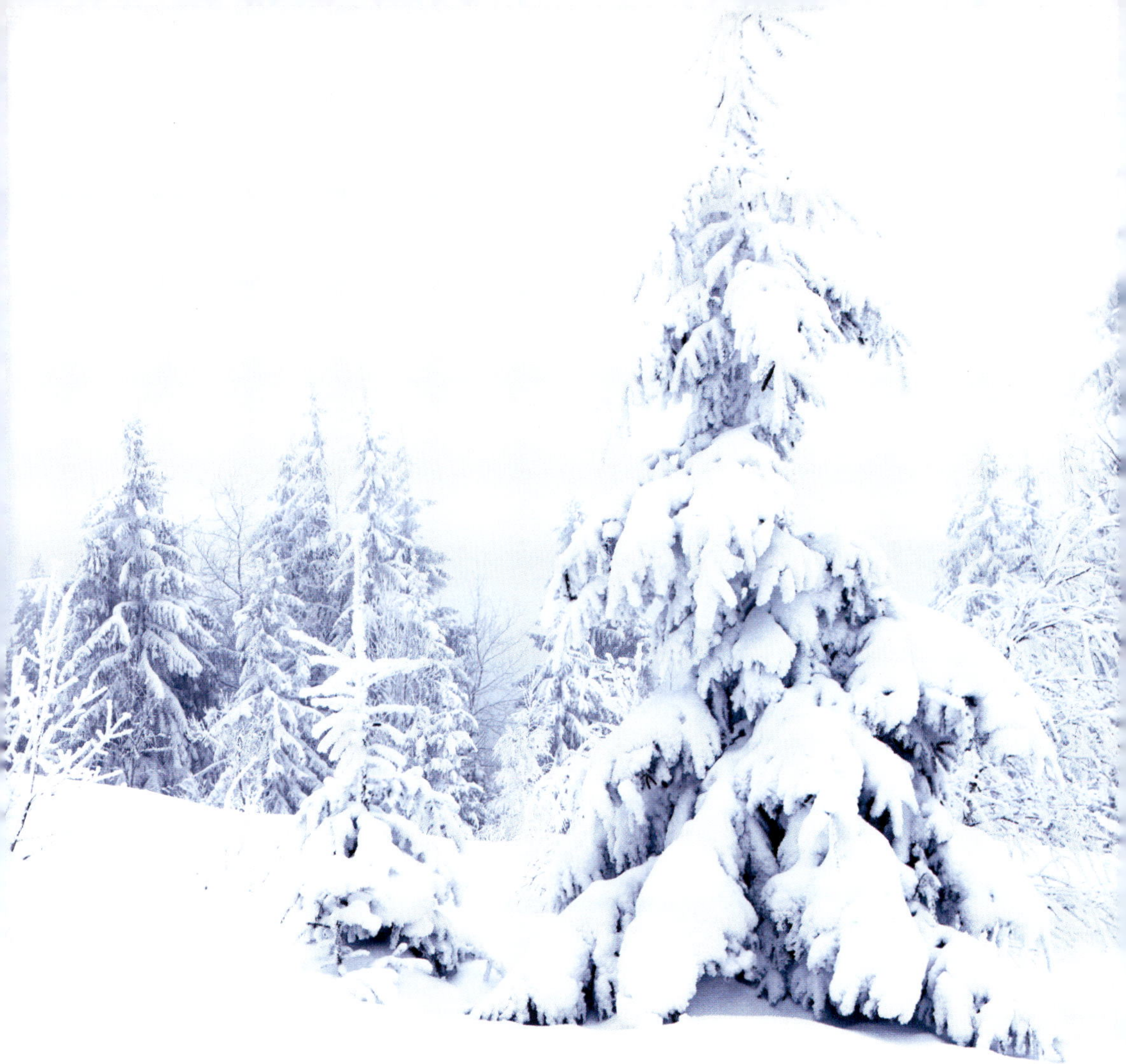

snow

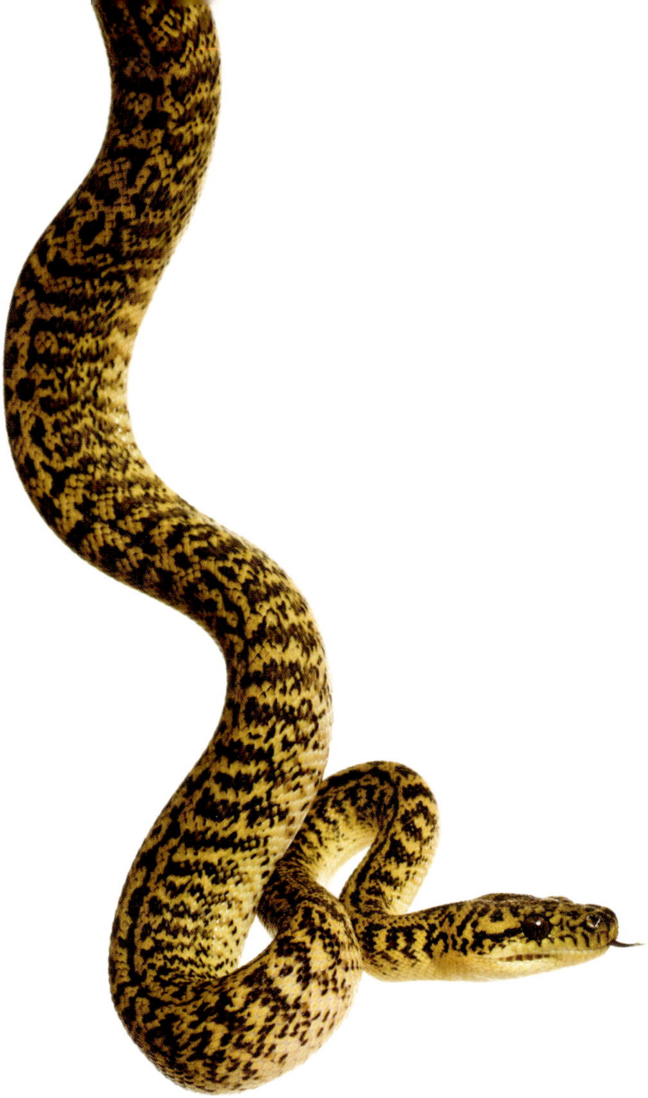

s s s s

s s s s

Ss

sun

sum

suds

dogs

stars

stamp

sky

snow